DECADE

BRYONY MARIE FRY

Collected Poems 2007—2017

Published by PRNTD Publishing 2017

Copyright © Bryony Marie Fry 2017

Bryony Marie Fry asserts the moral right to
be identified as the author of this work

ISBN 9780994462046

All rights reserved. No part of this book may be
reproduced, stored in a retrieval system, or transmitted
in any form, by any means, including mechanical,
electric, photocopying, recording or otherwise, without the
prior written permission of the publisher.

www.prntdpublishing.com

*For everyone who has
ever made me feel*

FOREWORD

By Chris Gill

Friend, PRNTD Co-founder and Independent Author

I first came across the work of Bryony Marie Fry when I saw her perform. It was at a small, crowded indie bar in Southampton, UK. I knew her a little at this point, from bumping into each other on nights out during my university days, so I was looking forward to hearing her play for the first time. Aside from the fact I knew she wrote her own songs and played guitar, I really didn't know what to expect from her performance.

Bryony, who always came across a little introverted when we spoke, presented something entirely different on stage. As soon as she opened her mouth to reveal a smoky, old school jazz voice; a cool confidence seemed to radiate from her. I was hooked. And have stayed that way ever since.

As the years have progressed, I've followed Bryony's creative endeavours from both close and afar. Whether it's her vibrant and unique art, or her work relating to overcoming addiction such as taking part in Channel 4's documentary film, *Addicts Symphony*; Bryony is never without an artistic project on the go.

Which is why I'm so excited to be part of the next chapter in her creative quest: co-publishing her debut book of poetry, *DECADE*. Containing prose written over the course of the last ten years, *DECADE* journals the personal, professional and spiritual growth of Bryony's journey into womanhood.

This journey sees Bryony overcoming hardship in *My Reality*: 'Life is clearer now / There's room to breathe', while *Dream* speaks of a 'beautiful place': 'I've seen a world of positive emotion / within the glimpse of a smiling face.'

But it's not all sunshine and blue skies. *Fractured Thoughts* details how Bryony will 'never be that innocent child I was back then,' while *Benevolently* asks a simple but powerful question: 'Have I a heart filled with rust?' This journey, from darkness to light, is a theme that runs through all of Bryony's work, whether it's her music, paintings or as seen in this book – poetry.

Much of this stems from the demons the artist has dealt with in the past, such as her experience with homelessness and a long battle with addiction. And just because Bryony has worked hard to overcome these ghosts, doesn't mean she's forgotten a single second of how they made her feel. This is why she's using them as fuel for her poetry, in a way that is as honest and vulnerable as her music.

It's not the first time Bryony has turned her own darkness into something positive and inspiring for others. When tortured musician Amy Winehouse sadly lost her fight with addiction back in 2011, Bryony – a huge fan of the late singer-songwriter – took the devastating tragedy as a sign. A sign that she needed to change her own path; which is exactly what she did.

Bryony's journey into recovery started then and continues now, as every recovering addict will know too well – it's an ongoing process that doesn't simply just disappear. Bryony has managed to find a way to tune into the deepest, darkest depths of her soul and pull from the experiences in her past to create art that is both captivating and inspirational for others – whether they're battling with similar demons or not.

I was living in London's Camden Town when Amy Winehouse was taken from us. Being the borough the singer resided, you could feel the sadness in the air. And, as a fellow fan, I was also hugely impacted by the loss – which is why I was so gratified to see Bryony turn what was such a sad outcome into something so positive and hopeful in her own life. Whether it was jumping from a plane or walking the Northern Line, Bryony has campaigned tirelessly for the Amy Winehouse Foundation, raising both money and awareness surrounding the effects of drug and alcohol misuse on young people.

It was both inspiring and a relief to see Bryony – who in many ways I remember as a slightly lost soul in Southampton – shedding a skin and growing into the strong and creative woman I always knew she was. Amy Winehouse saved Bryony's life. And I have no doubt Bryony will, if she hasn't already, save the lives of many others.

I remember Bryony handing me a demo of her music with a handcrafted sleeve not long after I first saw her play. Not only was this the sort of gesture of kindness that epitomises Bryony's personality, but a true symbol of her creative and DIY ethos that has remained with her throughout her entire career so far.

It's this DIY ethos that we at PRNTD identify with and support wholeheartedly. Which is why we're so happy to be bringing one of Bryony's many dreams to life with this beautiful and heartfelt book.

We hope you enjoy reading Bryony's poetry as much as we've enjoyed putting it together for you. And, on a personal note, I look forward to seeing what the next *DECADE* has in store for this bright and talented artist. Wherever it takes her, she will have me proudly watching from the sidelines. Rooting for her every step of the way.

PANDEMONIUM

I'm masking my emotions.
You're an excuse for me to cry.
I do not understand,
What's going on inside my mind.

I'm not happy if you are.
I'm nothing but a fallen star.
Something that once was,
Or never will be.
Just drift wood,
Far out at sea.

I cannot take it anymore.
There's no one to care,
No one to adore.
False reality approaches the door.
What am I here for?

DECADE

In a crowded room,
I am nothing but still air.
Unrecognisable.
This really can't be fair.

A cold, bitter-sharp wind,
Harshly caresses my face.
I could be everywhere,
Yet take up no space.

EVENTUALLY

A transit taken by surprise,
No, I don't want to compromise.
A stolen formation of butterflies.
Only single tears fall from your eyes.

Vast oceans capture the remnants of your flight.
Slowly drifting like an unwanted kite.
Swimming deep beneath the storm,
Your twinkling promises are torn.

Suddenly everything glows,
A prominent, black.
Silence my thoughts of,
Wanting you, back.

Aware of the reflection,
Of my demise.
I'm struggling to climb,
Towards your skies.

Am I not what inspires me to be?
Am I not what you want to see in me?
Broken as a fallen tree.
I'll disintegrate, eventually.

BRYONY MARIE FRY

MY REALITY

Distant skies,
Subtly change my mind.
Life is clearer now.
There's room to breathe.
I breathe out the hatred.
Cool, clean, sympathetic air,
Cleanses my lungs.

Inside out, I am free.
Free to believe my entwined thoughts,
Of what is real,
And what is not.
What is reality?

DECADE

As an autumn leaf,
Floats lovingly,
Towards a still lake.
Life is created.
Ripples gently awaken,
The cold reflective surface.
This is movement.

This is life.
This is reality.

CLUTTER

Life flows by,
Minutes seize my eyes.
Empty moments,
Fall between my fingers.
Feathers flutter,
No trivial clutter.
A breath, a shine,
I wish to find.

Roll away,
With the broken tide,
Blissful release,
From this forceful abide.
The petal falls.
With no intention to climb.
Whisper the words,
I long to hear.

Stamped out like a cigarette,
Embers burnt out,
No need to regret.
The truth may expose,
What I wish not to find,
But I do not care.

A whirlwind fluctuates,
Gathering lost intentions.
Speeding endlessly backwards,
Brought to denied attention.

To sit is to wait,
And to wait I do not.
To fall is a freedom,
A freedom I forgot.

Patrolling through,
Eyes of fire.
Destructive views,
Tear through desire.

DREAM

What is the use of a dream,
I wonder?
To escape from reality,
And discover?
A fictitious conclusion,
To your hopes and delusions.
What is the use of a dream?

I skip through the rain,
To disguise my tears,
Lonesome droplets,
Of tangible fears.
A diluted trail of aspiration,
Follows by my side.
My broken heart,
My devastation,
I can no longer hide.

From time to time I ask myself,

Why would I want to awake?

To a world so evil, so pretentious, so malignant, so fake?

But between the lies and deception,

There's such a beautiful place,

I've seen a world of positive emotion,

Within the glimpse of a smiling face.

BRYONY MARIE FRY

POCKETS

Holding hands within my pocket,
No wandering eyes can see.
I kept your smile inside my locket,
Within my heart for only me.

We stand surrounded in the dark.
Two lonely faces in the crowd.
I've loved you from the start.
Too afraid to say it out loud.

I see the steps on which we sat,
Where you smoked that cigarette.
You told me you wanted to hold me,
I looked at you so lovingly.

There is nothing you can recall.
It's as if it never happened.
Only my name left to ridicule.
I have no strength left to defend.

DECADE

My head is constantly tormented.
Your words repeat inside my mind.
I truly believed that you meant it.
Such a fool to think you weren't lying.

PALE ROSE

Pale pink rose,
Standing strong.
Withered petals,
Forgotten and forlorn.
An endless summer's sunlight,
Of which you mourn,
Yet buds will reappear,
Between your thorns.
Dreams will be revived,
And no longer remain torn.
Past burdens are a distant scorn.

Glow for me rose,
Your shaded petals of dawn,
For hope is in the soil you breathe.
Fear knows no way to return.

THE BEACH

A shadow,

Sweeps across the rock pool.

A sparrow,

You shouldn't be here, such a fool.

Go fly back.

Fly back to the place where you belong.

You shouldn't be here,

But you're not doing anything wrong.

This is the beach.

Where I come,

To be out of reach.

This is the beach.

I see a stone.

Pick it up and throw it.

Watch it go,

To the bottom of the sea.

You're unfit,

Unfit for the world up above.

Your beauty,

Is what the sea's,

Been dreaming of.

BRYONY MARIE FRY

FRACTURED THOUGHTS

Driving down that road,
With those familiar hedgerows.
So green are the leaves,
On those ever growing trees.
So many times they've seen me,
But how the years have really changed me.

Never will I be again,
That innocent child I was back then.

There are times I feel my fractured thoughts,
Of what love is supposed to be.
Lay like trampled flower beds,
In the deep dark sea of me.

DECADE

Driving down that road,
Up above me float the clouds.
Take with you the pain,
Of modern problems that remain.
As I look up at the sun,
I know a new chapter has begun.

Never will I be again,
That innocent child I was back then.

SEVENTEEN HUNDRED TO WATERLOO

Thoughts sweeping,

Wind rushing,

Past the cold steel shell,

That surrounds me.

So clinical,

So symmetrical.

Skies brooding.

Grey enveloping.

Swirls of evident nature encase me.

So perpetual.

So ostentatious.

Trees bowing.

Flowers retreating.

Speeding past structures of,

Brick and stone.

So haunting.

So beckoning.

Rain pounding.

Warmth resounding.

Surreal overlay of,

Broken conversations.

So intriguing.

So deceiving.

MILITARY SITUATION

I do not want to have to fight for your affections.
This is not a military situation.
You cannot keep giving,
And then taking away.
This is not a job,
Where you can pick and choose the days.

These feelings should come naturally.
They should be programmed automatically,
But they are not in your mentality.
You are forever disrespecting me.

Gone are the days,
When I believed you truly cared for me,
Grieved when you weren't there for me,
Cried when you lashed out at me.
Gone, are the days.

BRYONY MARIE FRY

SCARLET INFINITY

Outrageous to imagine.
Voices counteract the freedom.
Love requires no shadow.
No coveted path.
Explicitly enthralled.
Unadulterated delicious touch.
Eyes heavy.
Distant privacy.
One fingertip exalts the other.
No one cowers.

Fermenting love is so unkind.
Shallow complexities rule the mind.
This is no such love I see.
No sour traits before me.

How did they escape,
Erosion from reality?
Prerequisites of fertility,
Unbeknown,
Torments un-nurtured.
Unable to grow.

DECADE

Mangled modernity.
Romanticism lacking divinity.
No wait,
Could this be real?
Love perpetuating,
Through scarlet infinity.

BRYONY MARIE FRY

I MET MYSELF WITHIN A DREAM

At first it was a hazy memory.
A distant dream,
Lacking clarity,
But the colours became so vivid,
And your tears were somewhat, lucid.
You were brought right to me.
Your tiny feet stepped truly.
Your hair was golden white,
And your dress was claret red.
In my arms I held you tight,
And all your fears were put to bed.
Within that moment,
Something changed.
I saw you sleeping there,
Unchained.
I knew my inner me was free.
As your love swept over me.

DECADE

I DO NOT KNOW YOU

Sitting on the notions of what could be.
Taunted trails of light move esoterically.
Bitter tales of your Delphic dreams,
Of fluid truths and ancient streams,
But how can this be,
If I do not know you, nor you know me?

Mystic.
Like the motions of your mind.
Heavy.
Is the heart you left behind.
Unaltered is my life lately,
Yet still I think hypothetically,
But how can this be,
If I do not know you, nor you know me?

Your arcane eyes remain strange to me.
I conjure up illimitable possibilities.
Somewhat occult.
Thoughts brought to a halt,
But how can this be,
If I do not know you, nor you know me?

Enigmatic inclination.
Footsteps glide away.
Unexpected devotion,
Was that you who looked my way?
Fool me whilst I was dreaming,
Self-destructive and deceiving,
But how can this be,
If I do not know you, nor you know me?

BE PATIENT FOR LOVE

The pandemonium,
Of collaborated souls.
Both human and nature combined.
In anguish they're confined.
The energy is neither visible,
Nor defined,
Yet you can feel it quicken your pulse.

So many hearts,
Yet to be unearthed.
They trawl the streets,
Blind of the sky.
Where coaxing clouds,
And feathers fly.
A cerulean blue awaits,
To cleanse your hazy eyes.

To notice how the leaves retreat,
From vivacious bottle greens,
To that amber shade of orange-red,
So golden and serene.

DECADE

As nature mourns in cycles,

I've learned to follow how it grieves.

To reincarnate,

Pain and loss,

To beauty.

BROKE WITHOUT LOVE, BROKEN

Living life,

In tragic forms.

Misshaped.

Stagnant.

No escaping further tangents.

Each path leads to the same location.

Ulcerated.

Punctured.

As if in a mirrored room,

I see darkness in all who I meet.

Tarnished pain.

Dripping in proof,

Percentage.

Pungent.

Aching hearts.

Distended from acceptance.

This is what I believe.

Will anyone believe me?

Love.

Perhaps I do not deserve it.

Those tendrils of light.

A peaceful romance.

An unburdened, un-toiled emotion.

Perhaps I do not deserve it.

If all who I meet,

Seeps,

Drips,

That dirty pain.

That sullen cry.

Like a spider's fly.

Away.

Be gone.

Another plane,

A realm parallel,

To me,

You see.

I am the one who is crying.

PURGATORY

Like a bird stripped of air in mid-flight.
Pounding wings against a hostile, barren sky.
A bland purgatory.
Of which nothingness resides.

Silence isn't kind.
It ruptures wounds I left behind.
No protocol for pain.
A splinter hurts me when it pleases.
You were different yet the same,
Like a bleached bed of roses.
A haunting red bleeds from your stem,
The life escapes your soul,
Leaving only a bitter end.

SNOWDROP

Treat me like a snowdrop.
Innocent and wild.
Don't be naïve and wonder,
Why I won't stumble,
When you're in your darkest hour.

Treat me like a snowdrop.
Glowing through the mire.
Embracing winter's temptress,
Whilst you stand down and cower.

Treat me like a snowdrop.
Tread careful, tender ground.
For my petals are only strong,
When no pain is to be found.

BEAUTIFULLY BLUE

Floating in the blackened skies,
No earthly force to beseech me.
Torture hidden,
Corruption disguised.
A blanket of blue seas greet me.

I'm too far away to feel the hurt.
Too far away to see it.
Miles and miles above you, my world.
So beautifully blue.
Such an honest view.

You emanate magnificence.
Replacing hate with innocence.
So patient through your diligence,
Making all who lived significant.
To see that we as one can be,
So outwardly exquisite and free,
Gives hope to life beneath the clouds,
And faith in love to tortured crowds.

FIREWORKS

Fireworks.
Heat against the night.
You.
Always in my sights.
Just a night.
A fleeting love.
A momentary sense.
Of.
Lust.
In all forms.

Can a mind so passionately lust for love,
That love itself becomes diminished in its presence?

Just an object,
Of which once obtained,
Its strength begins to fizzle,
Like the fireworks?
Love has no visible flame,
Yet an endless organic fuel,
To keep the heat.
Energy.
Light.

NATURE RESIDES HERE

The concrete cracks.

Pushed back.

Splitting its,

Elephant skin façade.

The grey crumbles.

Nature prevails.

New shoots,

Of untarnished green,

Unreservedly guard,

Their new footings,

Roots revealing,

Their coiling tentacles,

Below the ground.

Small stems,

Wear tiny skirts of moss.

Velvety emerald,

Mixed with Spanish olive green.

Brambles trail,

Cut through the rust.

Degraded fences.

Derelict passes.

Weeds bloom beautifully,

Leaving tiny pavement carcases.

Dandelions and nettles,

Make their little temples,

As ivy cascades from above.

Together they eliminate,

Their man-made mantel,

To form a woven world,

Of which they can truly love.

HARD IRON GRIP

The hard iron grip.

Like barnacles.

Clenching.

Compressing.

Teeth to stone.

Dark energy fuels the fire.

Steam pressing.

Clamping.

My body is not my own.

As if wire crept under my skin.

Interlocking.

Muscles crushing.

Tension binding.

Jaw tightening.

A tiny heart lays breaking within each tooth.

Fractured displays of inward pain.

Dredged rivers.

Forgotten youth.

Dark energy fuels the fire.

Pain sharpens its blade,

With each word I speak.

I turn my cheek,

Towards the pyre.

BENEVOLENTLY

The lethargy of life within this moment.
A tidal of motivation, crushed.
Water swirling.
Energy dispersed.
The fickle contemplations.
Does your mind negotiate corners,
The same way that mine does?
Have I a heart filled with rust?

The desperation of hopeful conversation.
A whirlwind of fluttering delusions.
Heavy elements push the peace out from within.
Do you recoil,
Through fear of indulging me?
Have I an exterior,
Which proves my mind unworthy?

Take a tragedy,
Take your pick,
But you'll find no loose stitches at my seams,
For I am benevolently fused by the memories,
Of other people's sins against me.

NUMB TOMORROW

I cannot accept that I should not,
Feel the weight of the world,
Like a knot in a rope,
Holding anchor to ship,
Preventing the trip,
Where minds lose hope,
And hearts cannot float.

I cannot wake and wipe the tears,
Of a hundred thousand eyes.
I cannot take my hands in theirs,
Or stop them from their demise.
All that I can do is feel,
Caught as if a fish to reel,
A hook through my heart,
A hook made of steel,
And steel into rust,
And rust into dust,
Until emotions absorb,
Into that acidic salty orb,
A toxic ocean of fears,
Diluted by years,
Of pain and sorrow,
Until we are all numb,
Tomorrow.

THE WOLVES

Burn it all, take it away.

I have no need of you.

I've learned to live alone,

The wolves will fight me when I'm through.

Run from me, speak dulcet tones.

Cease my heart to beat.

I need not breathe your words,

Hungry mouths devour my pride,

Morsels fall towards my feet.

Hate all that I do,

Let it be your burden,

But is it me I'm talking to?

The wolves are hunting in circles,

There are no flowers left to bloom.

Black and white eyes,

Stripped of colour.

Piercing like ice against warm finger tips.

Shadows are closing in.

The wolves are here,

Now it's time to begin.

DECADE

NAVIGATE THE RAIN

I get anxious,
I can't sleep.
Take these thoughts,
Away from me.
Lift me high into a dream.
Teach me new beginnings.
The subtleties of freedom.
The contentment from within.
The friction of deception.
All of true love's notions.

I'm learning how to fly again.
Take my steps above the ground.
I'll let my soul navigate the rain.
The floods won't reach me when I'm found.

I won't revel in my fragility,
Or wallow in the negativity.
The visceral movements.
The pain is all too real,
But I can choose to close my eyes,
And witness the sunset of my mind's skies.
The giant fan coral of silhouetted trees,
These are my inner realities.

BRYONY MARIE FRY

WIRED AND ALONE

I know what it feels like,
To be wired and alone,
With nothing but your mind,
To make you feel so juxtaposed,
Between the darkness of your soul,
And the light that makes you whole.

When nothing is real,
And your fragility stands visible.
So solitarily lost,
And filled with dread right to the bone.

Don't fear me,
I am not your enemy.
I am nothing,
Without my clarity.
So rest with me a while,
Until the daylight steals all,
Of the demons taking hold.
Just let me love you irrevocably.

DECADE

I know what it feels like,

To wake up in the black of night,

With nothing but your beating heart,

To startle you with fright,

And all the scornful memories,

Of the nightmares oh so dreadfully,

Tearing your soul to rags,

Like a forgotten Fifties prom dress,

Courting of an age gone by,

Naïvety refined,

The ghost remains as you digress.

WAITING WISTFULLY

Waiting, wistfully.
Realising, reconciling.
My own heart turns against me.
Incinerate these idiotic fantasies.

Perpetual timing.
The stars are reclining.
The sky holds you close,
Yet it pushes me away.
I'm a distant dead light,
Empty interactions inside,
My mind.

Wandering affection,
Knows no bounds of love's deception,
Perhaps it's all a lie,
And these eyes were born to cry.
I'm still chasing chances,
Over your displaced glances.
It doesn't matter where I am.
It never has,
You won't take my hand.

DECADE

How do I express this?
How do I try to address it?
Residual success,
Within the hearts of nothingness.

If you felt the same you'd be here,
Challenging the night,
But others have you in their palms,
Like blackened crows in flight.

BRYONY MARIE FRY

ELEMENTS

Transgressions seem repressed,
As you touch my skin,
Undress.
My outer existence,
Reaching deep,
No resistance.

The heat.
I let your flames break through.
The raw element of you.
We wait together,
For horizons new.

Your presence makes me unafraid,
Yet burdens me,
Somewhat overlaid.
A jovial temperament,
Tarnished with the unknown.
The uncontrollable.
The threat of being left alone.

Borders to be crossed in unison.
Don't over analyse this feeling.
Don't try to work out the meaning.
Let it flow in person.
Truth resides within the emotion.

AWAKENING

Why do I have to be,
In this realm of idiosyncrasies?
A wealth of forsaken ideologies.
Why is it that I've laid this bed,
With sober sheets?
In a world where liquor soaked lives,
Creep.
Deep into my thoughts,
I cannot escape.
Eyes draped in melancholy,
Yet everyone stands idly by me.

Isolated by a choice,
To be concise in my demeanour.
A fortuitous response,
Unwanted like the noose,
Tied around my heart.
My art is beckoning a new beginning,
Yet choking all possibilities.
No time for healing.
I beg of you to leave me in peace.
Allow my soul its awakening.

DECADE

Small aspects overcloud,

Negativity has a louder voice.

Don't listen.

Let love be your shroud.

Don't think about your past vice,

Present in everyone else.

On the shelf,

You see,

An eternal sense of me,

From a time passed,

A youth dishevelled,

An unobtainable way of being,

So utterly carefree.

Free from self-conscious doubt.

All eyes are not on you,

Yet you feel them burning.

One drink would stop the yearning.

A mind full of clutter.

A noisy space.

A place to create an elaborate stutter.

A limbo in time.

Trapped and confined.

That's where I'll leave these thoughts behind.

A white room,

And a black box.

The key thrown into the abyss.

An emotional state,

I will not miss.

Meditate from me,

Become a heightened individuality.

Stones fall heavily.

Don't allow yourself to follow their path,

The aftermath,

Of self-disillusionment,

You insincerely make way for happiness,

Disguising as you express,

Your views on being strong.

That's not an emotion,

Just a longing.

A longing for freedom.

Free to merge with the rivers of society,

And not be the one who is constantly fighting,

Me.

THE FINAL 'EX'

I know you're out there getting,

Faded.

Jaded.

The clarity of the night made my,

Teeth shake.

I can hear your empty heart,

Beating.

Honest love runs through my veins.

Synthetic adrenaline.

Featherless wings.

You're terrified of falling,

Yet you pluck out the feathers.

Weathered.

Enamoured.

I could never be that toxicity.

I wouldn't want to be so acidic.

Prolific.

Pain.

DECADE

You separate yourself,

Segregate.

Disallow yourself to regenerate.

Incinerate habits.

Barriers between happiness.

There are other forms of fun,

Be at one.

Pace your breath.

Idolise sanctity.

No need to rush incessantly.

My voice is wasted.

You're emotionally disconnected.

I felt at fault.

I loved too much.

You weren't done.

Prolonged right of passage.

Justification.

Seeking gratification.

The desperation to be adored,

The adoration of one was not enough.

You needed more.

You needed answers from me.

You needed answers from within.

Sometimes if you stick around,

Watch the seasons come around,

With fingertips entwined,

Patience.

Dreamy finds.

All you require.

Typed.

Clear font.

Needs and wants.

Pessimism expired.

Revealed in a moment of lust,

But transformed into trust.

You'll find yourself surrounded,

Loneliness dumbfounded,

But you would not treat yourself to,

It.

Had to find solace in that next,

Drink.

It hurt me,

To see.

Unwanted fragility,

But they were more important than,

Me.

DECADE

I could not win you back,

But you see,

I am at peace now.

I know that I am worthy.

Your flaws could not outwit me.

Hiding.

I keep mine where all can see.

Discriminating.

I make it easy for you to judge,

Me.

I'll face the fact you did not want,

Me.

The drinks and lines were your priority,

Also your prerogative.

I was just dismissive.

Envious perhaps,

I live in fear of relapse.

To which you did not respect.

You were the noose around my,

Neck.

I'm in the minority.

A social incompatibility.

It was impossible for you to love me in my sobriety,

Like this.

You made me hate,

Myself,

Like this.

Affectionate degenerate.
Even your best friend told me,
You should come with a warning.
I'll leave you in my past.
Your mind travels too fast.
One day you'll slow the beat,
But not tonight, not this week.
I know you're out there getting,
Faded.
Jaded.

3AM

There's a stillness.
A critical forgiveness.
That moment in the night.
I lay here as my witness.
Unable to hear my sigh.
I listen for both.
My heartbeat transposed.
Lips sweet like chai.

The hour is magic.
I breathe out the tragic,
Lies I tell myself.
That I'm not worthy,
That I need help.

Collection.
Blackness.
Refraction of time.
Tangents.
Inhabitants of my mind.

DECADE

Phosphorous and feeble.
Past tense, plural.
Non-vacuous.
Space fuelled by desire.
Space filled by desire.
Space filled with my empire.
No longer disastrous.
No longer loveless.
There's a force behind my fire.

LEFT BEHIND

The cold pavement.
Rough to the touch.
Moss holding onto life,
Like an arrangement of cut stems.
The feel of the earth, do they miss it much?
Folding leaves, tattered hems.
The old torment of the knife.

That voice, like a memory.
The timbre soothes the melancholy.
A vice for a blue-hued mind.
Strike the amber-soaked sky.
A sepia face against the light.
Old photograph.
Tragic and visionary.
The rain did not fall that day.
The glow hauled from the moon's night.

DECADE

Blue eyes wear a uniform of grey.
Ashes shroud a non-forgotten smile.
Beside the heavy stone, life strives.
Tearing through the ground.
Emerald hearts and sodium clouds.
The irony of laying flowers.
Killing to represent the killed.
Sitting lost for hours.
Clocks filled,
With salty lashes.
Bewildered cries.

A soul disconnected is a soul rejected.
The boundaries of love and existence.
The heart remains persistent.
The word was never said.
The love cannot be accepted.

BRYONY MARIE FRY

THE CROOKED HOUSE

The crooked house that holds me.
That overwhelming feeling.
All consuming.
All revealing.
Laying with your own heartbeat.
Lies admits defeat.
Inside this crooked house.
Sheltered from doubt.
Hiding under torn blankets.
Cascading trinkets.
What. Once. Was.
The just. Because.
The dust floating in the light.
Never seeming to settle.
Anxious wings of an indigo night.
Fingertips so gentle.
Float inside the negative.
Colours turned inside out.
Inside the crooked house.
Forgive the faith that never found you.
Respect the mind that grounds you.

I WAIT BECAUSE I CAN

I'm waiting because I can be alone within these walls,
And know that love will one day grasp
My chest and pull my lungs deep.
Shallow breaths become steeped in resonating harmonies.
Freedom from my own atrocities awaits me.
I'll swim through clouds of ash like fire under water.
I'll bide my time until I have a daughter,
So I can teach her how to become a woman
With faith in life's imperfections,
How to close in on the stars and realise
That their lives are just like ours,
And that perhaps our energy shines into distant galaxies,
And people wish upon us to
Guide them through their tragedies.
How to be at one with the sky,
And that it's okay to cry,
To feel the weight of the world,
Like waves tumbling from waterfalls of hatred,
Because without hate,
Love would not know how to be sacred.

I AM NOT THE ROSE

I see your image early in the morning.

Gravitating the notions of perfection.

Every aspect deserves devotion.

I see your eyes wide like passion flowers.

Working effortlessly,

Like crystals shining.

Born to envelop my emotions.

Yet I am not the rose you wish to devour.

My beauty does not echo the waterfalls that you follow.

Their trails shimmering into lakes of purity.

My lake grows colder each day.

Not even a single tree to comfort its tainted shores.

I am not the depth you wish to explore.
Where life finds ways to reinvent survival.
Fighting against the inky black.
You did not see my silhouette,
But I am the pre-raphaelite revival.
Whilst you were standing idle.
You did not see my roots gaining ground.
My heart growing wild.
Like a meadow beckoning the breeze,
These flowers are sacred to me.
Each a reminder that I am worthy,
For we are not the same, you see.

BRYONY MARIE FRY

WHY ARE THE OTHERS ALLOWED TO BE?

Why are the others allowed to be?
The ones with eyes like vermillion suns,
Rippling along the horizon,
As the night entices,
All of the moons of the sky,
An expanse of civilised light.
Why are the others allowed to be?

Why are the others allowed to be?
The ones with hearts like lavender oceans,
Imploring the depths to rise,
Like new earth and new life.
Chartreuse and shining.
Why are the others allowed to be?

Why are the others allowed to be?
The ones with souls entwined,
With silver stars so crystalline,
As the clouds give birth to rain,
A regalia of oily pearls.
Why are the others allowed to be?

I HEAR MUSIC, I SEE ART

I hear music when I look at your hands,
I envision the sounds when you touch me.
My tears resonate fragility,
And you cannot feel the beat.

Maybe you are aware of my presence,
Upon this earth, my space in time,
Within the forests and the oceans.
Whisper the melody, until it all falls in line.

I see art in the way you hold your stare.
A collage of sun hazed memories,
Lacing together like vines in English hedgerows.
I paint our bodies dripping with colour.

BRYONY MARIE FRY

LIKE A CROW

That very same thought engulfs me,

Once more.

Like a crow standing alone,
Waiting for the company of darkness.
A sorrow bespoke for a heart like mine.

Once more.

I harness the words to cultivate a justification.
We are all in a state of relapse.
Forever succumbing to the notion of loneliness.
That defiant collapse into the arms of nothingness.

Once more.

MIDNIGHT MEETING

The detrimental capacity,
Like indigo collapsing.
Midnight meeting the Mariana.

Waiting as if water,
Captured in long exposure.
Exposing me.
The definitive.
Weak until enraptured.

Translucent yet floundering.
Pounding from the pressure.
No pleasure in purgatory.

I wait as if I am aware,
Like the moon longing for full light.
No respite from darkness.

ABOUT THE AUTHOR

With a mother who is an artist and a father who is a musician, it was inevitable that Bryony would forge a career in the creative arts. The materials to explore her artistic side were there right from the start, and due to learning the flute, penny whistles, bodhran and guitar at a very young age, Bryony found herself swept up in a traditional folk music environment. This had a profound impact on her current alternative psych/folk style of songwriting. She is now blending styles and genres with her cello, drum pad, electric guitar and electronic effects.

Bryony battled with addiction for many years and developed various health implications because of this, but she has now been sober for over five years, consistently raising money for the Amy Winehouse Foundation through both her artistic and musical ventures. She identifies with the late singer-songwriter on many levels, and hopes to encourage her legacy to live on, inspire, and educate.

Bryony currently resides in Bristol where she devotes her time to music, art and writing.

www.brightsmoke.co.uk

www.ingramcontent.com/pod-product-compliance
Ingram Content Group UK Ltd.
Pitfield, Milton Keynes, MK11 3LW, UK
UKHW041228200426
11947UKWH00035B/574